Descriptive text by A.N. Court

COLOURFUL ENGLAND

Jarrold Colour Publications, Norwich

'The Old Barn', Chiddingfold, Surrey. 1.
« La vieille grange » pris de Chiddingfold, Surrey. 1.
„Die alte Scheune" bei Chiddingfold, Surrey. 1.

London and the South-East

London is far more than the capital of Great Britain and Northern Ireland and one of the largest cities in the world: she has an indefinable character and charm of her own. In this great historic city the modern rubs shoulders with the old, the great and the small live side by side in pleasant harmony, and in every part of London's complex and busy life there is to be found a very genuine affection for her traditions, her fortunes and her prosperity. Today the face of London is changing. Everywhere great new blocks of offices and apartments are climbing towards the sky. Victorian and pre-war façades are giving way to the bold lines of modern architecture, old streets are being widened and new ones constructed. Yet essentially London retains her personality; the 'Beefeaters' still guard the Tower, the guard is still changed daily in the forecourt of Buckingham Palace and the cheerful Cockney still epitomises the unquenchable spirit of the capital.

South-east England broadly comprises the counties of Surrey, Kent, East and West Sussex, Hampshire, Buckinghamshire and Hertfordshire and those parts of Essex and Berkshire lying within the London commuter belt. The North Downs, extending across Surrey into Kent, and the South Downs, which reach from Hampshire into Sussex, are the salient features of the south of this region. Between the two chalk masses lies the Weald, a great bowl once covered with dense forest but today is rich in orchards, hopfields and market gardens. Hampshire contains within its boundaries the old cathedral city of Winchester, the great naval base of Portsmouth and the country's leading passenger port of Southampton. The coasts of Sussex and Kent are graced by a delightful succession of holiday resorts enjoying an equable climate. To the north of the Thames basin, with its many delightful riverside townships, rise the Chiltern Hills, cradling the Vale of Aylesbury. Hertfordshire, Buckinghamshire and Surrey, away from the London suburban area, are predominantly rural counties with many unspoiled villages and pleasant woodlands.

The Houses of Parliament (2) were completed a century ago and incorporate a part of the medieval Palace of Westminster. The imposing clock-tower houses the celebrated chimes; Big Ben, the hour bell, daily sends forth its message to the world that London is well and truly alive. The House of Commons was unfortunately practically destroyed in 1941 during a bombing raid, but has been rebuilt. Westminster Hall, with its magnificent hammer beam roof, was the scene of some of the most famous trials in British history. Buckingham Palace (3) was purchased by George III in 1762, rebuilt later by Nash, and since 1837 it has been continuously used as the official London residence of the sovereign. Facing the Palace at the end of the broad Mall stands the statue of Queen Victoria. The white marble memorial, surmounted by the winged figure of 'Victory', was unveiled in 1911. The imposing stone façade of the Palace was added by Sir Aston Webb in 1913. The Tower of London, for many years a royal residence and a prison, has stood by the Thames for nearly a thousand years. William the Conqueror built the massive keep which now houses a fine collection of armour. The security of the Tower is the responsibility of a military garrison and of the Yeoman warders or 'Beefeaters' (4) who wear a traditional sixteenth-century uniform. Units of the Brigade of Guards, comprising the Household Cavalry and the five regiments of Foot Guards, are normally stationed in London. The Household Cavalry, resplendent in their colourful uniforms and mounted on their magnificent horses, are an attraction which never fails to excite the admiration of onlookers. Each of the regiments of Foot Guards (5) – Grenadier, Coldstream, Welsh, Irish, and Scots Guards – has a distinguished record in military campaigns. St Paul's Cathedral (6) crowns Ludgate Hill in the historic square mile of the City of London. The present building, the third to stand on the site, was designed by Sir Christopher Wren. Although the external architecture is Classical in its conception, the interior follows the normal Gothic plan. The dome, perhaps the best known of London's landmarks, is 365 feet high, and beneath it is the celebrated 'whispering gallery'.

2

3

4

5

Le Parlement (2), vu du Albert Embankment, date du 19e siècle et renferme une partie de l'ancien Palais de Westminster. Buckingham Palace (3), acheté en 1792 par le roi Georges III, est la résidence principale de la famille royale depuis 1837. Les « Beefeaters » (4) qui portent toujours leur uniforme de l'époque Tudor gardent la Tour de Londres. Un détachement de Gardes à pied (5) défile le long du Mall à l'occasion d'une cérémonie traditionelle. La Cathédrale de St. Paul (6), qui couronne le sommet de Ludgate Hill, remplace une ancienne église détruite par le Grand Incendie de 1666.

Die Parlamentsgebäude (2), der Sitz der Regierung Großbritanniens, wurden im vorigen Jahrhundert errichtet und schließen einen Teil des mittelalterlichen Westminsterpalasts ein. Buckingham Palace (3) ist seit 1837 die Hauptresidenz der königlichen Familie. Für den Londoner, sowie auch den Ausländer, ist dieser Palast eine besondere Attraktion. Die „Beefeaters" (4) in ihrer traditionellen Uniform aus dem 16. Jahrhundert bewachen den Tower. Eine Abteilung Foot Guards (5) marschiert in voller Pracht den Mall entlang. Der St. Pauls Dom (6) krönt Ludgate Hill in der Innenstadt.

7

Even in Roman times Canterbury was an important meeting place, and it was here that St Augustine began his ministry and built the first cathedral towards the end of the sixth century. The Cathedral, the seat of the Primate of All England, was begun in 1070, but the present building is largely in Perpendicular style. There are many picturesque old houses (7) in the town. Royal Tunbridge Wells is situated in the west of Kent, near the East Sussex border. Its fame spread early in the seventeenth century when the town became a fashionable spa. The Pantiles (8) derives its name from the tiled paving of its elevated pathway. Before the sixteenth century, Chiddingfold, in Surrey, was famous for its glass, some of which adorns Westminster Abbey. Near Chiddingfold, on the edge of the Weald, are some of the oast-houses (9) which are a feature of this part of south-eastern England. Hopping time (10) is in September, when whole families of Londoners take up temporary residence in the hopfields and work long hours to gather the crop, and incidentally to earn good money. Ramsgate, once a subsidiary of the Cinque Port of Sandwich, is built on high ground and is a bracing holiday resort. Its firm sands, nearly a mile wide at low tide, are a paradise for children. Ramsgate Harbour (11) is a busy place and is especially popular as a yachting centre. Aylesford (12), to the north-west of Maidstone, is typical of the villages of mid-Kent. The fourteenth-century bridge spanning the Medway and the oldest over that river, was widened during the last century. An Iron Age cemetery was discovered here in 1886.

8

9

10

11

12

Vieilles maisons de Cantorbéry (7), dont la célèbre cathédrale est le siège du primat d'Angleterre. Les « Pantiles » à Tunbridge Wells (8), ville d'eau devenue célèbre au 17ᵉ siècle, sont des allées pavées de tuiles flamandes. Typiques de la région de la Weald sont les séchoirs à houblon (9) près de Chiddingfold, célèbre avant le 16ᵉ siècle pour ses verreries. La cueillette du houblon, (10) qui a lieu en septembre, est souvent effectuée par les Londoniens. Le port de plaisance de Ramsgate (11), autrefois l'un des Cinque Ports est maintenant lieu de villégiature. A Aylesford (12) on remarque le pont du 14ᵉ siècle et un cimetière de l'âge de fer.

Von Canterbury, das schon in römischer Zeit Bedeutung hatte, begann St. Augustin seine Mission. Neben dem Dom im Perpendikel-stil findet man viele malerische Häuser (7) in dieser Stadt. Der Name „The Pantiles" (8) im einstmals berühmten Kurort Tunbridge Wells leitet sich von dem mit Ziegeln gepflasterten Weg her. In der Nähe von Chiddingfold, von wo das Glas der Westminster Abbey stammt, stehen einige der für diese Gegend typischen Oast-Häuser (9). Im September kommen ganze Familien zur Hopfenernte (10). Als Zentrum für Yachten ist Ramsgate Harbour (11) sehr beliebt. Die Brücke von Aylesford (12) ist die älteste über den Medway.

13

14

15

Le front de mer à Eastbourne (13), ville touristique qui a été dévelopée au 19e siècle. A Brighton, la reine des plages du Sussex, le Pavillon Royal (14) fut construit par le futur Georges IV. A Mayfield, petite ville intéressante pour ses monuments anciens, se trouve un vieux moulin (15). A Midhurst il est agréable de flâner le long de la Rother (16). Whitley, (17) avec ses maisons à toit de chaume, est l'un des nombreux pittoresques villages du Surrey. Les « Waggoner's Wells » (18) à la limite du Surrey et du Hampshire, sont cinq étangs au milieu des bois.

Die Promenade von Eastbourne (13) ist eine der schönsten entlang der Südküste. Der „Royal Pavillion" (14) von Brighton, der Königin unter den Urlaubsorten von Sussex, ist eines der außergewöhnlichsten Bauwerke von England. In der Nähe von Mayfield steht eine reizende alte Mühle (15). Midhurst ist ein Zentrum für Wanderungen im bewaldeten Hügelland von Sussex oder entlang des Flusses Rother (16). Eines der reizenden Dörfer von Surrey ist Whitley (17) mit seinen strohgedeckten Häusern und der netten Kirche. Die „Waggoner's Wells" (18) sind fünf Teiche inmitten von Wäldern.

Eastbourne was known to the Romans but its development, dating only from the last century, is due in no small measure to the influence of the Dukes of Devonshire, on whose land the town is built. The sea-front (13) is unrivalled on the south coast; it is dignified and spacious and in places divided into several levels. Beachy Head, nearly 540 feet above sea-level, is the most frequented spot on the South Downs. No one can dispute that Brighton is the 'queen' of Sussex resorts. Two piers, a promenade over five miles long and every conceivable form of entertainment make the resort the most popular in the south. The Royal Pavilion (14), surely the strangest edifice in England, is a symbol of the affection which the Prince of Wales, afterwards George IV, felt for the town. Near Mayfield, a charming little town on the road from Maidstone to Eastbourne, stands a fine old mill (15). There are some interesting old houses and the remains of an arch- bishop's palace in Mayfield. Midhurst is a convenient base for rambling along the wooded downs of western Sussex or for more leisured strolling by the River Rother (16), where there are a number of fine yew trees. A mile to the north of the town are the remains of Eastbourne Priory, to which the parish church of Midhurst was formerly attached. To the north is Cowdray Park, one of the few places in the country where polo is still played. Witley (17) is one of the many charming villages of Surrey. Its beautiful thatched cottages and attractive church make it a most charming place. Waggoner's Wells (18), on the borders of Surrey and Hampshire, consists of a series of five pools in a woodland setting not far from Hindhead. Although its name suggests that this might be a place where waggoners watered their horses, this would be a long way from the truth. Waggoner is, in fact, a corruption of Wakener, who was a master ironworker. In Tudor and Stuart times and probably much earlier the Weald had a flourishing iron industry, and water power was often used to drive the hammers, the ponds thus becoming known as hammer-ponds.

16

18

17

Richmond got its name from Henry VII, who thus commemorated his original title of Duke of Richmond. Edward III, Henry V and Henry VII all had palaces here, but only a gateway and the Wardrobe Court of the last one survive. Richmond has two fine parks: Richmond Great Park and the Old Deer Park. The former, nearly 2,300 acres in extent, is well stocked with deer and cattle, and by the Woodland Pond are attractive beds of azaleas (19). The Old Deer Park belies its name, for there are now no deer here; instead it is used for sport and as the venue for the Royal Horse Show. The spirit of yesteryear lives on in the old villages of the Isle of Wight such as Godshill (20), with its old-world thatched cottages and a splendid Perpendicular church which once belonged to a priory. The church has a number of tombs dating from Tudor days which are notable for their fine carving. Bournemouth, Dorset's leading seaside resort, is a comparatively modern town, having grown into its present considerable size within the last hundred years. The bay, on which the resort lies, is enhanced by wooded chines which reach down to the shore and give Bournemouth a particular charm. The chines were formed by the wearing away of softer rocks through the action of a stream. Of several which Bournemouth possesses, Alum Chine is the largest and most imposing. The sea-front (21) flanks a beach of fine clean sand, and four tides a day make the beach ideal for bathing. The New Forest was once considerably larger than it is today, extending from the Solent to the Wiltshire border. The word 'forest' did not originally mean a profusion of trees, but rather uncultivated tracts of land where game abounded. This is particularly true of the New Forest, where the woods are broken by stretches of marsh and heath. Wild ponies (22) are one of the principal attractions. They are extremely hardy and fend for themselves throughout the year. All, however, are privately owned, the owners paying dues for the right to graze their animals in the Forest.

19

20

21

22

Richmond, qui reçut son nom d'Henry VII, a deux beaux parcs. Dans le Grand Parc, bien pourvu en cerfs et bétail, on peut admirer des parterres d'azalées (19). Le Parc du Vieux Cerf est utilisé pour le sport. Avec ses cottages et son église perpendiculaire, Godshill (20) est l'un des villages typiques de l'Ile de Wight. Bournemouth (21) est une ville assez moderne et la plage la plus en vue du Dorset. Des arêtes boisées viennent jusqu'à la mer et agrémentent la baie. La New Forest est un ensemble de bois et de landes. Les troupeaux de poneys sauvages (22) y attirent les touristes.

Herrliche Azaleen (19) schmücken den Woodland Pond im Richmond Great Park, der im Gegensatz zum Old Deer Park voll von Wild und Rindern ist. Godshill (20) auf der Insel Wight mit seinen Strohdächern und der Kirche im Perpendikelstil hat die Atmosphäre früherer Zeiten erhalten. Bournemouth hat durch seine bewaldeten Schluchten einen besonderen Reiz. Der Strand entlang der Stadt (21) ist wegen seines feinen Sandes und der vier Gezeiten pro Tag ein herrlicher Badeplatz. Stets im Freien lebende wilde Ponies (22) sind eine große Attraktion des New Forest.

23

25

24

26

Marlow (23) est une vieille ville-marché du Buckinghamshire où habita le poète Shelley. On peut y voir un pont suspendu. Bourne End (25) est un centre touristique au confluent de la Wye et de la Tamise. Plus en aval sur la Tamise se trouve Cookham (26). Maidenhead (27), à la limite des bois de Cliveden, a un passé important. De là on explore les rives de la Tamise. Non loin de là, la forêt de hêtres de Burnham (24) appartient à la Cité de Londres. La résidence royale de Windsor (28) fut commencée comme forteresse par Guillaume le Conquérant. L'intérieur en est très riche.

Marlow (23), mit seiner graziösen Hängebrücke über die Themse, ist ein alter Markt von Buckinghamshire. An der Mündung des Flusses Wye liegt Bourne End (25); etwas flußabwärts, gegenüber der bewaldeten Cliveden Reach, ist Cookham (26). Maidenhead (27) ist beliebt als Ausgangspunkt für Ausflüge in die Themselandschaft. Vier Meilen von hier ist der als Burnham Beeches (24) bekannte Wald, der 1879 von der City of London gekauft wurde. Das Bild der Stadt Windsor wird vom Schloß (28), der königlichen Residenz, geprägt. Seine Prunkgemächer bergen wertvolle Möbel und Gemälde.

27

Marlow (23) is an old market town of Buckinghamshire with a history going back to Saxon days. The graceful suspension bridge over the Thames was built about 1836. Shelley lived for a time at Marlow, and his house is still standing, though it has been considerably altered. Passing through Marlow Lock we arrive at Bourne End (25), another popular riverside resort; here the River Wye, otherwise known as the Bourne, enters the Thames. A short way downstream on the Berkshire bank is Cookham (26), opposite the wooded stretch known as Cliveden Reach. Cliveden Woods, part of the Astor estate now in the care of the National Trust, extend as far as Maidenhead (27) which is a fine centre for exploring the Thames countryside. Although Maidenhead is to all outward appearances a very modern and lively town, it has a considerable history, the first charter having been granted by Elizabeth I. Four miles from Maidenhead are the six hundred acres of woodland known as Burnham Beeches (24), purchased by the City of London in 1879. The ancient town of Windsor is dominated by its Castle (28), famous as one of the royal residences. Like so many of our island fortresses, Windsor Castle was begun by William the Conqueror, who constructed a central keep and surrounded it by a fortified wall. The stone castle was begun in the time of Henry I and continued by succeeding monarchs. The State Apartments contain valuable furniture and paintings, including fine carvings by Grinling Gibbons and Henry Phillips. St George's Chapel, the great glory of Windsor, stands today as it was when completed in 1528. The Chapel contains the stalls of the Knights of the Garter.

Bien que restaurée, l'église de Sandridge (29), construite au début du 12e siècle, a gardé son air ancien. La Cathédrale de St. Alban's (30), abbaye normande d'origine, a la nef la plus longue d'Angleterre. Le lac de Connaught Water (31) est dans la forêt de Epping, achetée au domaine royale par la Cité de Londres. Le moulin à vent de Stanstead Mountfichet (32) date du 18e siècle. Le long des quais de Maldon (Essex) on peut voir amarrées les péniches navigant sur la Tamise (33).

Die Kirche von Sandridge (29) ist noch immer von einem Hauch der Vergangenheit umgeben. Wie sie hat auch der Dom von St. Albans (30) römische Ziegel in den Mauern. Sein gotisches Mittelschiff ist das längste von England. Im Westen des Epping Forest liegt der schöne See Connaught Water (31). Eine der besterhaltenen Windmühlen des Landes steht in Stanstead Mountfitchet (32). Am Kai von Maldon liegen malerische Segelbarken (33) vor Anker.

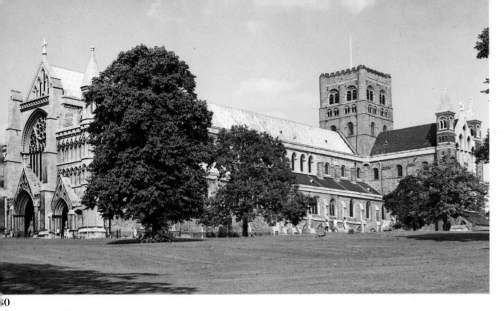

Sandridge Church (29) was built at the beginning of the twelfth century when the parish belonged to St Albans Abbey. Although it has been considerably restored it still retains an atmosphere of the past. The chancel arch is built with Roman bricks, and the stone screen dates from the fourteenth century. St Albans Cathedral (30), too, has Roman bricks in its structure, but it was originally a Norman abbey with later additions. The Gothic nave is the longest in the country. Considerable necessary restoration was undertaken nearly a century ago and much of the external architecture is now unashamedly Victorian Gothic. St Albans was a Roman city called Verulanium on the important Watling Street and extensive remains are still to be seen. Epping Forest was once the Royal Forest of Waltham, a hunting ground for the monarchy. Extending over 5,600 acres, Epping Forest was acquired for the public by the City of London in 1862 and opened by Queen Victoria. Connaught Water (31) is an attractive lake to the west of Epping New Road. Stansted Mountfitchet lies to the north of Bishop's Stortford. The windmill (32), one of the best preserved in the country, dates from the end of the eighteenth century. The earthworks near the station are believed to be the remains of the castle of the Mountfitchets who owned the township in Norman days. Maldon, at the head of the Blackwater Estuary, has a fifteenth-century Moot Hall containing portraits of Elizabeth I, Queen Anne and George III. The parish church is remarkable for its thirteenth-century triangular tower. Picturesque Thames sailing barges (33) are often to be seen alongside the quay.

Lincoln Cathedral. 34.
La cathédrale de Lincoln. 34.
Der Dom von Lincoln. 34.

East Anglia and the East Midlands

East Anglia may be described as a great peninsula, with a sea coast extending from the Wash in the north-west to the estuary of the Blackwater river in Essex. The western boundary is less easy to define. Both historically and geographically there are good reasons for the inclusion of eastern Cambridgeshire and northern and eastern Essex. Though the East Anglian countryside is generally low-lying, it is wrong to suppose that it is as uniformly flat as the Low Countries, with which it has sometimes been compared. Gently undulating pasture, wooded hills and delightfully picturesque river valleys present a constantly changing landscape, and although the rural scene predominates one is never far from one of the busy and pleasant market towns where old traditions are wisely preserved amid the more modern trends of life. East Anglia is predominantly a farming region, and the emphasis of its economy is essentially agricultural. Especially important is the growing of sugar-beet and fruit.

Several counties may conveniently be grouped under the title of the East Midlands. The most southerly is Bedfordshire, where market gardening is the principal rural occupation. Luton, the largest centre of population, was once world-famous for its straw hats, but is now principally known for the manufacture of cars, and in addition, for its airport. East of Bedfordshire is Northamptonshire, whose county town of Northampton is noted for the manufacture of footwear. Further east lies western Cambridgeshire, which is low-lying and drained by the Great Ouse and Nene. Northwards lies Lincolnshire, one of England's larger counties, with its rich fenland devoted to fruit-growing and the raising of bulbs. Leicestershire is divided by the Soar, a tributary of the Trent, with Charnwood Forest on its eastern flank. Nottingham, the county town of its shire, was once one of the chief Danish towns in England. One area of Nottinghamshire, called the Dukeries, forms part of Sherwood Forest, the scene of the legendary exploits of Robin Hood.

35

36

3

Clavering (Essex) (35) semble avoir eu une certaine importance car on y découvert les ruines d'un château fort. La Vieille Maison du Siège à Colchester (36), ville dont l'histoire remonte jusqu'à l'époque romaine. Birdbrook (37) est l'un des villages typiques de l'Essex. On peut y voir de vieilles maisons, une église normande et des ruines romaines. La Cathédrale d'Ely (38) fut commencée en 643 et poursuivie à l'époque normande. Vus des jardins, la chapelle de King's College et Clare College à Cambridge (39). L'architecture de la chapelle fait l'émerveillement des touristes.

Clavering (35) dürfte einst ein bedeutender Ort gewesen sein. Das elisabethanische Old Siege House (36) in Colchester, das angeblich die älteste registrierte Stadt Großbritanniens ist, spielte eine große Rolle in der Belagerung im Jahr 1648. Birdbrook (37) mit seinen malerischen alten Häusern und der normannischen Kirche ist typisch für Essex. Der Dom von Ely (38) stammt aus dem frühen 12. Jahrhundert; die ungewöhnliche Laterne wurde als Ersatz für den 1322 eingestürzten Turm errichtet. Von den „Backs" (39) hat man einen herrlichen Blick auf die Kapelle des King's College.

From the geographical standpoint northern Essex has close affinities with East Anglia, and although the countryside is generally undulating, nowhere does it exceed 500 feet in height. Clavering (35), some four miles east of Newport, must once have been a place of some importance as the remains of a former castle have been discovered close to the church. Colchester claims with some justice to be the oldest recorded town in Great Britain. It was about A.D. 43 that Colchester first became a Roman colony and it grew to become one of the most important towns in Roman Britain. Colchester Castle, built by the Normans, is believed to stand on the site of a Roman temple. Among other interesting buildings in the town is the Old Siege House (36), an Elizabethan building which played a prominent part in the great siege of 1648. Typical of the many charming villages of rural Essex is Birdbrook (37), with picturesque old houses and a Norman church; among the monuments is one commemorating a certain Martha Blewitt who had nine husbands in the seventeenth-century, and another to Robert Hogan who had seven successive wives! The foundation of Ely Cathedral (38) is very old, the original building having been begun by St Etheldreda in 673. The present church dates from the early years of the twelfth-century, but something was amiss with the usual excellence of Norman building, for in 1322 the central tower fell and severely damaged part of the nave and choir. The unusual lantern-tower was built in its place. King's School, Ely, originally a monastic foundation, numbered Edward the Confessor among its pupils. King's College Chapel and the magnificent Palladian building of Clare College are seen to advantage from 'The Backs' (39), the gardens on the river frontages of the Cambridge colleges. King's College Chapel was begun in the reign of Henry VI and continued under his successors. The magnificence of its architecture, the marvellous fan vaulting and medieval glass are a perpetual source of wonder and admiration.

38

39

Beaucoup des villages du Suffolk ont gardé leur caractère d'autrefois comme Chelsworth (40) avec ses cottages à poutres apparentes. Coddenham (42) date de l'époque romaine et son église du 13ᵉ siècle. Flatford Mill (41) est dans la basse vallée de la Stour, où Constable naquit et peignit. Southwold (44) est connu pour son phare et son église du 13ᵉ siècle. A Letheringham dans la haute vallée de la Debden on peut voir un moulin à eau (43). Lowestoft (45), la ville la plus à l'est d'Angleterre, est un centre de villégiature.

Chelsworth (40) und das viel ältere Coddenham (42) sind zwei attraktive Dörfer im fast unverändert gebliebenen Suffolk. Flatford Mill (41) sieht heute fast genau so aus wie es der 1776 in der Nähe geborene Maler Constable dargestellt hat. Das nette und ruhige Southwold (44) hat seinen Leuchtturm direkt in der Stadt. In Letheringham steht eine ausgezeichnet erhaltene Wassermühle (43) von East Anglia. Lowestoft (45), die östlichste Stadt Englands, ist ein beliebter Urlaubsort und ein bedeutender Fischerei- und Schiffbauhafen.

42

43

44

45

Suffolk has changed but little over the centuries, and many of its villages still retain an atmosphere of yesteryear. Chelsworth (40), between Sudbury and Stowmarket, has a number of well-preserved half-timbered cottages and an old church with a fourteenth-century canopied tomb. Coddenham (42), about three miles east of Needham Market, is an equally attractive village, but is probably much older, as it is recorded as having been called Combretonium by the Romans. The thirteenth-century church here has a double hammer-beam roof and an alabaster panel of the Crucifixion. The lower part of the valley of the River Stour is known as 'Constable Country', for it was here that the celebrated painter worked and had his home. Constable was born at East Bergholt in 1776 near Flatford Mill (41), which looks today remarkably as it does in his famous painting. Southwold (44) is quiet but charming, with its lighthouse unusually situated actually in the town. The Perpendicular parish church, one of the finest in the country, was built in the fifteenth century. It was intelligently restored about 1867, and both exterior and interior are of great merit. Picturesquely situated on the upper reaches of the River Debden, Letheringham possesses one of the old water-mills (43) of East Anglia in a fine state of preservation. Lowestoft (45) holds pride of place as the most easterly town in England. It is not only a popular holiday resort but also an important fishing and ship-building port. The 'scores' – narrow passages winding down to the Denes – are an interesting feature of the older part of the town.

46

49

Norwich, la plus grande ville du Norfolk, est connue pour sa cathédrale (46) de style normand. Great Yarmouth est une ville animée et centre d'attraction de la côte. Ici on voit la Jetée Britannia (47). Sheringham (48), sur la côte septentrionale, est une centre de pêche aux crabes. Sandringham est l'une des résidences royales. Le château de style élisabetain (49) est entouré de magnifiques jardins et attire de nombreux visiteurs. La rivière Ant (50) est l'une des rivières des « Broads » qui s'étendent entre Norwich et la côte.

Der Dom von Norwich (46)—hier mit Pull's Ferry abgebildet— ein Kleinod dieser alten und faszinierenden Stadt, ist eine berühmte normannische Kirche. Am Fluß Ant (50), einem Teil der Norfolk Broads, steht How Hill. Great Yarmouth bietet alle möglichen Vergnügungen, unter anderem erstklassige Varietévorstellungen, auf dem Britannia Pier (47) und dem Wellington Pier. Kleine Boote stehen am Strand von Sheringham (48) zum Krebsfang bereit. Sandringham House (49) aus dem Jahr 1890 ist die königliche Residenz in Norfolk.

Norwich, the largest town in Norfolk and one of the oldest and most fascinating cities in England, has many new buildings and modern streets but still preserves much that is old. Norwich Cathedral (46) is one of the most celebrated Norman churches in Great Britain. The nave is the second longest in England, and the 315-foot-high spire is exceeded only by that of Salisbury. Between Norwich and the coast are the 200 miles of navigable rivers and shallow lakes which are collectively known as the Broads. In summer these waterways are thronged with pleasure craft; by the River Ant (50) stands How Hill, now belonging to the Norfolk Education Committee. Great Yarmouth has been compared with Blackpool as the resort which caters for everybody. Indeed there is every possible amusement and diversion, unrivalled golden sands, an extensive promenade and two piers. Both the Britannia Pier (47) and the Wellington Pier have modern theatres where first-class variety is presented during the summer months. On the north coast of Norfolk are Cromer and Sheringham (48), both well known for fresh crabs which are caught close inshore by small boats. Cromer has a fine Perpendicular church with an imposing tower. Sandringham (49) is the Norfolk home of the Royal Family. The impressive mansion in Elizabethan style was built in 1870 and is set in magnificent grounds in which also stands the little church which is visited by thousands every year. The interior of the church has an impressive silver altar and other fine furnishings, as well as many royal memorials. Members of the Royal Family attend services when in residence at Sandringham House.

Woburn Abbey est situé dans un vaste parc. L'intérieur, comme la chambre de la Reine Victoria (51), est très riche. Luton Hoo (Bedfordshire) (52) date du 18ᵉ siècle et abrite de nombreuses œuvres d'art. Le village de Hilton est situé entre deux voies romaines et l'on y trouve des cottages à toit de chaume (53). L'église d'Hemingford Grey (54) sur l'Ouse, fut commencée par les Normands. On dit que sa tour du 15ᵉ siècle est tombée et gît au fond de la rivière.

Eines der Prunkgemächer in der vielbesuchten Woburn Abbey ist das prachtvolle Schlafzimmer der Königin Victoria (51). Die Villa birgt auch eine unerreichte Sammlung von Canalettos Gemälden. In einem riesigen Park steht Luton Hoo (52) mit der Wernher Sammlung von Kunstwerken in seinem Inneren. Das reizende Dorf Hilton mit seinen strohgedeckten Häusern (53) liegt zwischen zwei Römerstraßen. Hemingford Grey (54) am Fluß Ouse hat eine wunderschöne Kirche.

51

52

53

54

Woburn Abbey, the seat of the Marquis of Tavistock, is undoubtedly the most visited of the stately homes of England. The abbey which once stood on the site was pulled down by the fourth Duke of Bedford, and the present mansion dates largely from the eighteenth century. The State Apartments, among which is Queen Victoria's Bedroom (51), are magnificent and the collection of Canaletto's paintings is unrivalled. Part of the huge park has been converted into a Safari Park. Luton Hoo (52) is an eighteenth-century house which was originally designed by Robert Adam. Set in a park of 1,600 acres, it houses the Wernher Collection of works of art, including rare paintings and personal possessions of the former Russian royal family. The village of Hilton in Cambridgeshire lies between two Roman roads, Ermine Street and Via Devana. The church, although of the fifteenth century, has Roman brickwork incorporated into its masonry. There are charming thatched cottages (53) and a turf maze which was constructed by a certain William Sparrow in 1660. Hemingford Grey (54) lies beside the River Ouse in Cambridgeshire in the heart of England. Its beautiful church was begun by the Normans and has several features of the period. The tower dates from the fifteenth century, but its spire was blown down over two hundred years ago and is reputed to lie beneath the waters of the river. There is a thatched cottage in the village which was built in Tudor times and has been inhabited ever since.

55

La façade ouest de la cathédrale de Peterborough (55) date du début du 13e siècle. L'ensemble du bâtiment est d'architecture normande à la base avec additions ultérieures. Castle Ashby (56) est l'un des châteaux imposants d'Angleterre. Situé dans un vaste parc il fut commencé au 16e siècle et terminé au 18e. L'intérieur est aussi impressionnant que l'extérieur. Preston est un bon exemple des charmants villages du Leicestershire. Certains de ses vieux cottages (57) datent des Stuarts et son église possède des mosaïques et des chandeliers rapportés d'orient. Leicester a une histoire très ancienne comme le prouvent ses vestiges romains. Le Guildhall (58) est d'époque médiévale.

Auch der Dom von Peterborough weist massive normannische Architektur auf. Seine herrliche Westfront (55) stammt aus dem 13. Jahrhundert. In einem schönen Park mit einer drei Meilen langen Buchenallee steht das imposante Schloß Ashby (56). In sienem Innern befindet sich eine große Halle mit einer Spielmannsgalerie. Preston mit seinen alten Landhäusern (57), die zum Teil in die Zeit der Stuarts zurückreichen, ist ein entzückendes Dorf in Leicestershire. Die lange Geschichte von Leicester in den Midlands zeigt sich in der Jewry Wall, einem Teil der römischen Stadtmauer, zwei römischen Gehsteigen und dem Forum. Die reizende alte Guildhall (58) diente dreihundert Jahre lang als Rathaus.

The history of Peterborough is the history of its cathedral which grew from the seventh-century monastery of Medeshamstede, the 'house in the meadows'. Both the exterior and the interior have massive Norman architecture, with additions from the succeeding centuries. The arches of the nave are still supported on their Norman pillars, and high above is a painted wooden roof, the only Norman roof in an English cathedral. The West Front (55) of the early thirteenth century is magnificent, rivalling those of Salisbury and Wells. The 'New Building', a fifteenth-century chapel, encloses the twelfth-century apse. Castle Ashby (56) is one of the stately homes of England. Set in a fine park with a beech-lined avenue three miles in length, it was begun late in the sixteenth century and completed in the eighteenth. The interior is as impressive as the outside and has a Great Hall with a minstrel gallery. As the representative of the many delightful villages of Leicestershire, Preston has much to commend it. There are some delightful old cottages (57), some of which go back to the days of the Stuarts. Among the treasures to be found in the old church are two pieces of 500-years-old mosaic from the Church of St John the Baptist at Constantinople and candlesticks from Damascus. Leicester, one of the busiest cities of the Midlands, has a very long history. Excavations have revealed that the Romans had a forum here, and they built a wall round the town, part of which, the Jewry Wall, is still to be seen, as are two Roman pavements. The fine old Guildhall (58), dating from the late fourteenth century, was used as the Town Hall for three hundred years. Next to it is the Mayor's Parlour, built during the reign of Henry VII, which contains a fine chimney-piece. It is believed that Shakespeare's players may have performed in the Great Hall.

56

58

57

59

60

61

Newark (Nottinghamshire) est une ancienne ville de relais. Le château (59) fut assiégé par Cromwell et seule subsiste l'enceinte du 12ᵉ siècle. Wollaton Hall (60), musée d'histoire naturelle de Nottingham, est un manoir élisabétain aux décorations extérieures flamandes. La Maison du Conseil à Nottingham (61), bâtie en 1927 dans un style 18ᵉ siècle, donne sur la place du marché où se tenait autrefois la foire aux oies. Au printemps le Lincolnshire est tapissé de tulipes (62). Le riche sol des Fens permet la culture des fleurs à bulbes.

Vom Schloß von Newark (59), das von Cromwells Truppen zerstört wurde, nachdem es drei Belagerungen überstanden hatte, stehen nur mehr die äußeren Mauern. Die elisabethanische Villa Wollaton Hall (60), die außen flämischen Einfluß zeigt, unterscheidet sich durch den erhöhten Saal von anderen Bauwerken des 16. Jahrhunderts. Hinter dem riesigen Marktplatz von Nottingham (61), wo früher immer die berühmte „Goose Fair" abgehalten wurde, steht jetzt das 1927 erbaute Council House. Ein herrlicher Teppich von Tulpen (62) breitet sich im Frühling über die Landschaft von Lincolnshire.

Newark, which once had Gladstone as its Member of Parliament, lies on the main road from London to the North. Of its twelfth-century castle (59) only the outer walls survive, and the inside has been laid out as a garden. The castle was destroyed when Cromwell's troops forced its surrender, after it had successfully withstood three sieges. King John is reputed to have died in the castle. Newark, as befits a former coaching town, has many old inns, notable among them being the Saracen's Head. Wollaton Hall (60), the ancestral home of the Willoughby family on the outskirts of Nottingham, is a magnificent Elizabethan mansion set in a noble park. Its elevated central hall distinguishes it from other examples of sixteenth-century architecture. The external decoration has distinct Flemish characteristics. Wollaton Hall was acquired by Nottingham Corporation in 1924 and now houses the city's Natural History Museum. Nottingham today ranks high as a manufacturing centre, with special emphasis on lace, hosiery, tobacco, medicines and bicycles, but in the tenth century it was one of the chief Danish towns of England, and it is reasonable to suppose that some kind of fortification existed on the hill on which Nottingham Castle now stands. The castle was restored in 1875 and is now a civic museum and art gallery. Nottingham's huge market square, where the famous 'Goose Fair' used to be held, is now an open space in front of the Council House (61), built in 1927 in a style reminiscent of the eighteenth century. Springtime in Lincolnshire (62) sees the countryside covered with a magnificent carpet of tulips in hundreds of varieties and in every possible variation of colour – bringing pageantry to the levels of the fens and making the scene reminiscent of Holland across the North Sea. The rich soil of the fenlands is particularly suited to the growing of bulbs, and a thriving industry has developed. Visitors come from far and near to marvel at the splendour of the bulb fields, and few depart without taking with them a floral memento.

62

Knaresborough, North Yorkshire. 63.
Knaresborough sur la rivière Nidd. 63.
Knaresborough am Fluß Nidd in North Yorkshire. 63.

The North

The four counties of South Yorkshire, West Yorkshire, North Yorkshire and Humberside cover a wide area and together offer a fine variety of North Country scenery. Here are to be found the great and dynamic industrial regions of Leeds, Bradford and Sheffield and the large port of Kingston-upon-Hull. Presenting a great contrast to these busy cities are the beautiful Yorkshire Moors and Dales, the North Wolds and the great plain of York with that incomparable city to entrance the visitor, as well as a fine stretch of coast with many charming resorts, both large and small. Durham shares with Northumberland rich coal deposits and has heavy industries; but the western part of the county is hilly, and it was here that the people of the Stone and Iron Ages made their homes. Relics of their occupation can be found in the museums of the county. To the east of Durham lie the small counties of Cleveland and Tyne and Wear, both busy industrial regions. Northumberland, lying between the Cheviot Hills and Durham and bounded on the west by Cumbria, is the most northerly of the English counties. In the south-east is a large industrial area, but, like Durham, much of the surface of the western part consists of sparsely populated moorland broken by charming river valleys. The coast, too, is largely unspoiled and boasts some pleasant holiday resorts with fine sands.

Cumbria is bounded on the north by the Cheviots and the fertile plain of Solway and on the east by the Pennines. The heart of the county includes the great area of the Lake District, with Scafell Pike, the highest mountain in England, and this is truly one of the most lovely parts of our islands. Away from the industrial areas Lancashire boasts the western slopes of the Pennines and a fine sea-coast, with several of the country's leading seaside resorts. Merseyside and Greater Manchester also have rural attractions away from Liverpool and Manchester, and, further south, Cheshire has many fine houses, built with money from those industrial centres, amidst its widely diversified scenery.

It is impossible in a few lines to do justice to the City of York, for it is one of the most historic cities of England. From the medieval city walls there is a fine view of the towers of the Minster (64), which was begun in the eleventh and completed in the fifteenth century. It is notable for the splendour of its external architecture and for the beauty of its stained glass. The 'Five Sisters' window is ranked as the finest of its kind in the world, and the east window is probably the largest medieval window in existence. Castle Howard (65) was built for the Earls of Carlisle to the designs of John Vanburgh, and it took thirty years to complete. The interior is rich in works of art and in the furnishings and decoration, including paintings by Tintoretto and Canaletto. In the grounds stand Classical statues and monuments. The Yorkshire Dales – the entrancing valleys of the rivers which come down from the Pennines to unite and find their way into the North Sea through the great Humber Estuary – are particularly lovely in their upper reaches. The visitor to Wharfedale is sure to be charmed by the village of Grassington with its long weir (66). The old town of Whitby clusters around its ancient harbour (67) at the mouth of the River Esk. The modern resort lies on the west cliff, and on the other side of the river is the old town with the ruins of Whitby Abbey high above. The Abbey was founded in 658 by Hilda, the daughter of the King of Northumbria, but the original church was destroyed by Danish invaders. It was refounded by the Normans and suffered its final desecration at the Dissolution. Only parts of thirteenth- and fourteenth-century work remain. Captain Cook sailed on one of his earliest voyages from Whitby harbour, and the ships he used for his first voyage round the world were built here.

64

65

66

67

Vues du haut de l'enceinte médiévale, les tours de la cathédrale de York (64) qui fut commencée au 11e siècle. Castle Howard (65) dans le North Yorkshire renferme de nombreux œuvres d'art comme des tableaux de Le Tintoret et Canaletto. Le parc est agrémenté de statues et monuments classiques. Le plan d'eau de Grassington (66) est un exemple des très beaux paysages que l'on peut admirer dans les hautes vallées du North Yorkshire. A l'embouchure de l'Esk, le vieux Whitby est regroupé autour de l'ancien port (67) tandis que la ville moderne s'étend à l'ouest.

Das Münster von York (64) ist wegen seiner prachtvollen Außenarchitektur und seiner Glasmalereien berühmt. Das „Five Sisters" Fenster gilt als das schönste dieser Art auf der Welt. Schloß Howard (65), das innerhalb von 30 Jahren nach dem Plan von John Vanburgh erbaut wurde, ist reich an Kunstschätzen. Grassington mit seinem langen Wehr (66) ist ein entzückendes Dorf in den Yorkshire Dales. Der alte Hafen (67) an der Mündung des Flusses Esk ist der Kern von Whitby. Eine Ruine ist alles, was von der 658 hier gegründeten und von den Normannen wiedererbauten Abtei noch zu sehen ist.

68

70

69

Près du village isolé de Langdon Beck (68) la Tees forme une cascade haute de deux cents pieds—Caldron Snout. Le Musée de Bowes (69) fut construit sur le modèle d'un château français de la Renaissance. Il a une riche collection de tapisseries. La Cathédrale de Durham (70) se dresse dans un méandre de la Wear. La ville elle-même est une romantique surprise au milieu d'une région très industrielle. Le château de Bamburgh (72) était la residence du roi de Northumbrie. Il est de style normand et domine le village de façon impressionante. L'Ile Sainte (71), au large de Beal, détient son nom d'un monastère construit là au 7e siècle.

Die Straße von Middleton nach Alston führt durch das Dorf Langdon Beck (68). Das nach seinem Erbauer benannte Bowes Museum (69) im Stil der französischen Renaissance enthält eine Sammlung von Gemälden, Keramik- und Elfenbeingegenständen und wertvollen Wandteppichen. Der Dom der romantischen Stadt Durham (70) steht hoch auf einem Hügel; besonders bemerkenswert ist seine Kapelle der Neun Altäre. Bamburgh ist jetzt ein nettes Dorf, doch das Schloß (72) erinnert noch an die Bedeutung der einstigen Königsstadt. Drei Meilen von der Küste von Northumberland entfernt liegt Holy Island (71) mit Schloß Lindisfarne.

71

The road from Middleton in Teesdale to Alston, one of the loneliest in the North, ascends the upper valley of the Tees and comes to the village of Langdon Beck (68). From here a moorland road, which reaches a height of over 2,000 feet, goes to St John's Chapel, linking Teesdale and Weardale. Two impressive water-falls break the course of the Tees; Caldron Snout, near Langdon Beck, is a series of cataracts falling some 200 feet, while High Force, nearer Middleton, is a single fall of 70 feet. John Bowes, who lived for some time in France, built the imposing museum (69) which bears his name near his home at Barnard Castle. The Bowes Museum, which is in the style of a French château of the Renaissance period, was opened in 1892. The collection includes paintings, ceramics, ivories and priceless tapestries. The City of Durham is an un-expected delight, for this romantic old town is situated in the midst of a highly industrialised region. Durham Cathedral (70) stands high on a hill enclosed by the great loop of the River Wear. The interior of the Cathedral is enriched with fine Decorated work; especially noteworthy is the Chapel of the Nine Altars which replaced the original aspe. Bamburgh, once a royal city, is today a pleasant village, but an imposing reminder of its former importance is the Castle (72), perched high on a basalt rock overlooking the sea; it was once the principal residence of the kings of Northumbria. The present building, dating chiefly from Norman times, has been considerably restored but still presents an impressive spectacle. Like Bamburgh, Lindisfarne Castle on Holy Island (71) is built on a precipitous rock. It dates from the sixteenth century and was later restored as a private residence. The name of Holy Island, situated about three miles off the coast of Northumberland, opposite Beal, derives from the fact that a monastic establishment was set up here in the seventh century by St Aidan who came from Iona.

73

The three reaches of Ullswater (73), England's largest lake, have a total length of seven miles, and in its broadest part the lake is a mile wide. The scenery is extremely varied, with mountain and tree-clad hills encircling the blue waters. Patterdale, at the head of the lake, has associations with St Patrick, to whom the village church is dedicated. From Ashness Bridge (74) there is a fine panorama of Derwentwater, one of the loveliest lakes in the British Isles. Its surface is broken by a number of tiny islands, the best known of which is St Herberts, where the hermit and disciple of St Cuthbert is supposed to have lived. One of the curiosities of the lake is an island which apparently floats; through the action of natural gas the vegetation sometimes appears above the surface. The lakes in the western part of the district present a wilder and even more romantic appearance than those in the more frequented valleys. Crummock Water and Buttermere have a personality of their own, and like Loweswater (76) are preserved with their surroundings by the National Trust. Coniston Water is the third largest of the lakes, measuring about five and a half miles in length. Coniston Fells brood over the village and the lake, and their lord is Coniston Old Man (77). John Ruskin had his home, Brantwood, overlooking the lake and he is buried in the churchyard of Coniston village. Rydal Water (76), like Grasmere, is inseparably associated with Wordsworth, who spent the last thirty-seven years of his life at Rydal Mount. Dove Cottage, Grasmere, where the poet lived for several years, has been preserved as it was in Wordsworth's time.

74

75

Le lac de Ullswater (73) est le plus grand d'Angleterre. Le paysage qui l'entoure est très varié. Du pont d'Ashness (74) on a une belle vue sur le lac de Derwentwater. Il est parsemé d'îles miniscules dont l'une est très curieuse car par un phénomène gazeux elle semble flotter. Le lac de Loweswater (76) est comme plusieurs autres protégé par le National Trust. John Ruskin avait une maison donnant sur le lac de Coniston (77) et est enterré dans le cimetière du village. Rydal Water (75), comme Grasmere, est inséparable de Wordsworth, qui y passa les trente-sept dernières années de sa vie.

Ullswater (73), der größte See Englands, ist von abwechslungsreicher Landschaft umgeben; er ist an einer Stelle eine Meile breit. Von der Ashness Brücke (74) hat man einen herrlichen Blick auf den See Derwentwater, dessen Kuriosität eine treibende Insel ist. Loweswater (76) und seine Umgebung ist wie einige andere Seen Naturschutzgebiet. Von Brantwood, dem Heimatort John Ruskins, sind der Berg Coniston Old Man (77) und Coniston Water gut zu sehen. Rydal Water (75) ist wie Grasmere untrennbar mit Wordsworth verbunden, der seinen Lebensabend in Rydal Mount verbrachte.

76

77

78

79

80

Levens Hall (78), au sud de Kendal, est un manoir du 12ᵉ siècle, fortifié au Moyen Age et modifié à l'époque élisabétaine. Les jardins sont à remarquer. Dans le nord-ouest d'Angleterre le contraste est grand entre les villes industrielles et la campagne environnante, comme le prouve cette photo prise près d'Abbeystead (79) dans la vallée de la Wyre. « Hall-i'-th'-Wood » (80) est la maison qui fut occupée par Samuel Crompton à Bolton, centre d'industries textiles. Blackpool (81), le plus grand centre balnéaire d'Angleterre, a un front de mer de plus de dix kilomètres.

Levens Hall (78), ein Schloß aus dem 12. Jahrhundert, ist wegen seiner herrlichen Gärten und der Schnitzereien im Innern bekannt. Der Nordwesten Englands bietet einen überraschenden Gegensatz zwischen Industriegebiet und reizender Landschaft. Das Wyretal in der Nähe von Abbeystead (79) am Fuß der Penninen ist typisch dafür. Hall-i'-th'-Wood (80), das jetzt als Museum dient, wurde im 15. Jahrhundert erbaut. Blackpool (80) mit seinem sieben Meilen langen Strand ist der größte Urlaubsort am Meer. Sein Wahrzeichen ist der berühmte 500 Fuß hohe Turm.

Kendal is the southern gateway to the Lake District, but it is well worth exploring for its own sake. In the castle, now only a ruin, was born Catherine Parr, the last wife of Henry VIII. Five miles to the south-west Levens Bridge spans the River Kent and near by stands Levens Hall (78). The Hall, a manor of the twelfth century, was fortified in the Middle Ages. In Elizabethan times the existing buildings were incorporated into a fine mansion. The interior is notable for its wealth of carving and the gardens for their fine topiary. The hard-working people of north-west England – whose homes are in the great cities of Liverpool and Manchester and in the numerous smaller industrial towns which seem to overflow into each other – do not have far to go to find rest and relaxation. Indeed, one of the surprising things about the north-west is the contrast between the industrial area and the charm of the countryside. Typical of the rural scene is the valley of the River Wyre near Abbeystead (79) at the foot of the Pennines but only ten miles from the busy M6 motorway. The story of Bolton is the story of wool and cotton, for this large Greater Manchester town has earned its livelihood for 800 years by weaving and spinning. Bolton's most famous son was Samuel Crompton, who lived from 1758 at Hall i' th' Wood (80) which had been let out in tenements during the eighteenth century. The house was built in the fifteenth century, but the stone additions were made over a hundred years later. The house was restored by the first Lord Leverhulme and is now a museum. Blackpool (81), the largest seaside resort in the United Kingdom, has a sea-front extending for seven miles and every possible amenity for the holidaymaker. Its dominant feature is the famous tower, rising to a height of 500 feet and incorporating a ballroom, a menagerie and an aquarium. Facilities of all kinds contribute to the claim of Blackpool to be the most up-to-date resort in Europe. Even in autumn the town is still full, for the elaborate illuminations attract thousands of sightseers.

81

82

Adlington Hall (82) se trouve près de Prestbury. Il est en partie du mi-16e siècle et de l'époque élisabétaine. On dit que Handel y a joué de l'orgue. A Chester, ancien camp romain et ville fortifiée, les touristes admirent les vieilles maisons et les auberges comme le « King's Head » (83). Avec ses maisons blanchies à la chaux le petit village de Wincle (84) est typique du Cheshire. L'église d'Astbury (85) est curieuse; l'une de ses tours, datant du 14e siècle, est séparée du corps principal—l'autre est du 15e siècle.

Der ursprüngliche Teil der Adlington Hall (82) stammt aus der Mitte des 10. Jahrhunderts, aber der Großteil dieses Fachwerkgebäudes ist aus der elisabethanischen Zeit. Händel soll hier die Orgel gespielt haben. Chester war, wie der Name verrät, einst ein römisches Lager. Das Gasthaus „King's Head" (83) ist eines der vielen herrlichen alten Häuser. Wincle (84) ist typisch für die netten Dörfer von Cheshire. Astbury hat eine ungewöhnliche Kirche (85) mit zwei Türmen; nur ein Torbogen verbindet einen der Türme mit der Kirche.

83

84

Adlington Hall (82) lies north of Prestbury by the River Bollin. The original part of the mansion dates from the middle of the sixteenth century, but most of the half-timbered building is of Elizabethan date. The front portico and adjoining wing date from the eighteenth century. The Great Hall has a notable hammer-beam roof with flying angels. Handel is said to have played the organ here. Adlington Hall suffered during the Civil war when it was attacked by Parliamentary forces. Chester, the county town of Cheshire, was, as its name suggests, an important Roman camp. In those days and in later medieval times the city had protective walls, parts of which still stand. The red sandstone cathedral, dating from the twelfth century, was originally a Benedictine abbey. It has considerable monastic remains and is notable for its fine woodcarving. Chester has many fine old houses and inns of which The King's Head (83) and the Falcon are notable examples. Typical of the charming little villages of Cheshire is Wincle (84), situated some six miles north-east of Congleton near the Staffordshire border. Lime-washed walls are a feature of houses in this part of England as are black-and-white 'herring-bone' timbered houses; one of the finest examples of these is Little Moreton Hall, near Congleton, a moated house which was built in the sixteenth century. The long gallery and the Great Hall are of particular interest. Astbury's unusual church (85) has two towers; one dating from the fourteenth century but resting on Norman foundations stands apart from the main body of the church to which it is linked by an archway; the other was added a hundred years later. The spire on the older tower is a much later addition. The interior is notable for its medieval stalls and for the fine Jacobean woodwork of the pulpit, pews, altar rails and roof.

Tredington, Warwickshire. 86.
Tredington dans le Warwickshire. 86.
Das Dorf Tredington in Warwickshire. 86.

The West Midlands

The West Midlands extend from the borders of Wales to the Peak District at the southern end of the Pennines, and include the great metropolis of Birmingham, England's second largest city, and the busy towns of the Black Country. In the north of Derbyshire is the Peak District, a region which belies its name, for there is no single summit but rather an area of rough moorland with Kinder Scout (2,083 feet) as its highest point. Three wonderful river valleys, the Derwent, the Wye and the Dove, flow through parkland and gorge to join the Trent. Fine old houses, the caves of Castleton and Matlock and the splendour of old churches all contribute to the charm of a delightful county. Staffordshire includes not only the Black Country and the Potteries but also considerable areas of rural charm, especially the dales adjoining Derbyshire and the heathland of Cannock Chase. Stoke-on-Trent was formed in 1910 by the amalgamation of five towns. Its most famous citizen was Josiah Wedgwood the potter. Lichfield, the birthplace of Dr Johnson, possesses one of our finest medieval cathedrals.

The River Severn separates the northern part of Salop from the more hilly south, where the Clee Hills rise to a height of 1,800 feet. The county of West Midlands contains Birmingham, Britain's second largest city, with its famous centre the Bull Ring, and Coventry with its fine modern cathedral and imaginative shopping precinct. The county of Hereford and Worcester is drained by the Rivers Wye, Severn and Teme and their tributaries and has extensive fruit-growing areas, especially in the Vale of Evesham. The Malvern Hills rise close to the centre of the county and to the west are the mountains of Powys. The town of Worcester has long been famous for its pottery, and Hereford has a Norman castle and a fine cathedral. Warwickshire is Shakespeare's county. Everywhere one is conscious of the influence of England's greatest poet and dramatist, and his birthplace at Stratford has become a place of pilgrimage. Warwick, the county town, and the famous spa of Leamington are also of considerable interest.

87

Chatsworth House (87) was originally built in the sixteenth century; the present mansion dates from the time of Charles II. The magnificent formal and informal gardens, with their cascades and fountains, are one of the principal attractions. The famous *trompe l'œil* painting of a violin on the door of the music room still deceives many who see it for the first time. The construction of three great reservoirs has changed the face of Derwent Dale. The Derwent (88), Howden and Ladybower reservoirs are complementary, the last named being the largest in England. Almost every visitor to Derbyshire makes at least one visit to Dovedale (89), where the river has worn its way through the limestone rocks and carved them into fantastic shapes, some of which have been given romantic names, such as 'Lion's Head,' the 'Twelve Apostles' and 'Dovedale Church'. Monsall Dale (90) is part of the River Wye which sweeps round Fin Cop, a hill just over 1,000 feet high. A waterfall is an added attraction to the two-mile-long dale which is at its loveliest in early summer. Built by Bess of Hardwick at the end of the sixteenth century, Hardwick Hall (91) is a wonderful example of an Elizabethan mansion. The interior is no less striking than the exterior, especially the High Great Chamber, the principal reception room. Fifteen miles to the west stands Haddon Hall (92), constructed in the sixteenth and seventeenth centuries on a Norman foundation. The State Apartments include the famous Long Gallery with beautiful bay windows. The gardens and park, through which flows the River Wye, are justly famed.

88

91

89

92

90

Les magnifiques jardins de Chatsworth House (87) sont l'un de ses principaux attraits. La Vallée de la Derwent (88) fut changée par l'aménagement de trois plans d'eau réservoirs. Dovedale (89) est une autre de ces vallées creusées profondément par la rivière. La roche y a pris parfois des formes curieuses, judicieusement baptisées. Monsall Dale (90) est courte mais très attrayante; une cascade ajoute à son charme. Hardwick Hall (91), construit au 16ᵉ siècle, est un très bel exemple de manoir élisabétain. Haddon Hall (92) est entouré d'un trés beau parc.

Die prachtvollen Gärten mit ihren Kaskaden und Springbrunnen sind die Hauptattraktion des Chatsworth House (87). Derwent Reservoir (88) und zwei andere große Staubecken haben das Derwent Tal stark verändert. In Dovedale (89) hat der Fluß im Kalkgestein fantastische Formen geschaffen. Monsall Dale (90) ist ein Teil des Flusses Wye. Das Innere der elisabethanischen Villa Hardwick Hall (91) ist ebenso eindrucksvoll wie ihr Äußeres. Haddon Hall (92) wurde im 16. und 17. Jahrhundert auf normannischen Grundmauern errichtet.

The pride of Lichfield is its three-spired cathedral (93), one of the smallest but undoubtedly one of the love-liest of our cathedral churches. The present building of red sandstone is in Early English and Decorated style and dates from the thirteenth century, though the foundation is six hundred years older. The West Front is adorned with over one hundred effigies of apostles, prophets, kings, angels, saints and bishops, with the figure of Christ high above the central window. Inside there is a wealth of wonderful carving and fine glass, and the whole building is a tribute to tasteful design and craftsmanship. Dr Johnson was a native of Lichfield and the house in which he was born is now a museum devoted to his memory. Few better examples of Victorian half-timbered houses exist than Wightwick Manor (94), some three miles from Wolverhamp-ton. The estate was purchased in 1887 by Samuel Mander, whose son, Sir Geoffrey, donated it to the National Trust shortly before the last war. Claverley (95) is in Salop, just over the Staffordshire border. It is a picturesque place with half-timbered old cottages and a church of red sandstone in which are some thirteenth-century mural paintings and two fonts. The vicarage dates from the fifteenth century, and the old village cross still stands. A mile to the north-east is Ludstone Hall, a Jacobean mansion. Less than a mile to the south of Craven Arms in Salop, Stokesay Castle (96) is a beautifully preserved example of a thirteenth-century fortified manor. The gatehouse, with its overhanging upper storey, was built in Tudor times. Between the three-storied south tower and the smaller north tower are a banqueting hall and a drawing-room. On the far side of the moat stands the church, notable for its seventeenth-century gallery and three-decker pulpit.

Avec ses trois flèches, la Cathédrale de Lichfield (93), bien que petite, est l'une des plus belles d'Angleterre. La façade est ornée de plus de cent statuettes et l'intérieur est décoré richement et avec goût. Le Manoir de Wightwick (94), près de Wolverhampton, est l'un des meilleurs exemples de maisons victoriennes à poutres apparentes. Claverley (95), petit village du Salop, a gardé des vestiges de différentes époques comme sa cure du 18e siècle, ses vieux cottages et son église à décorations murales du 13e siècle. Au sud de Craven Arms se trouve un manoir fortifié, qui s'appelle Stokesay Castle (96) et qui date du 13e siècle.

Die dreitürmige Kathedrale von Lichfield (93) ist trotz ihrer geringen Größe eine unserer schönsten Kirchen. Die Westfront ist mit über hundert Bildern von Aposteln, Heiligen, Königen, Bischöfen und Engeln geschmückt. Das Innere ist reich an Glasmalereien und Schnitzereien. Wightwick Manor (94) ist eines der schönsten viktorianischen Häuser. Claverley (95) in Salop ist ein malerischer Ort mit alten Fachwerkhäusern und einer Kirche aus rotem Sandstein. In dieser sind Wandgemälde aus dem 13. Jahrhundert und zwei Taufsteine zu sehen. Stokesay Castle (96) ist ein gutes Beispiel eines befestigten Ritterguts. Das Pförtnerhaus mit dem überhängenden Oberstock stammt aus der Tudorzeit.

L'Allée de l'Église à Ledbury (97) est remarquable pour ses maisons à poutres apparentes. L'église est de style Normand. Weobley (98) est le même type de village. Là, l'église est du 14e siècle. Birtsmorton Court (99), maison à poutres apparentes, entourée d'un fossé, date du 14e siècle. Rien ne reste du château qui a donné son nom au village de Elmley Castle (100). Commencée par les Normands, la Cathédrale de Worcester (101) fut achevée au 14e siècle.

Die Church Lane von Ledbury (97) in Hereford und Worcester ist bekannt wegen ihrer schwarzweißen Fachwerkhäuser. Auch das Bild von Weobley (98) ist von solchen Häusern beherrscht. Birtsmorton Court (99) ist ein von einem Graben umgebenes mittelalterliches Haus. Das Dorf Elmley Castle (100) hatte einst, wie der Name sagt, ein Schloß. Der Dom von Worcester (101) wurde von den Normannen begonnen, doch das jetzige Bauwerk gehört dem 14. Jahrhundert an.

97

98

100

99

101

The black-and-white timbered houses in Church Lane Ledbury (97) are a famous feature of this charming town in the county of Hereford and Worcester. The old Market Hall, a seventeenth-century building in the square, is listed as an ancient monument, and the Feathers Hotel dates from Elizabethan days. The church is Norman, Decorated and Perpendicular, the thirteenth-century Bell Tower being separate from the rest. Half-timbering is also a feature of Weobley (98) on the Leominster to Brecon road; the church here is principally of fourteenth-century date with an impressive tower and spire. On the outskirts stands The Ley, a notable example of a sixteenth-century manor-house which is now a farm. Birtsmorton Court (99), in the southern region of Hereford and Worcester, is a good example of a moated medieval timber-framed house, the oldest parts of which go back to the fourteenth century when the cruciform church was also built. As its name implies, the village of Elmley Castle (100) once had indeed a castle, but only a few grassy mounds now remain. The Queen Elizabeth Inn, however, commemorates a visit paid by that monarch, and the church has monuments to the Savage family who occupied the castle for many decades. Worcester Cathedral (101), on the left bank of the River Severn, was begun by the Normans, but most of the present building dates from the fourteenth century. The principal monument is the tomb of King John, with the earliest royal effigy in the country.

102

103

La Moat House à Hampton-in-Arden (102) est un exemple des maisons à poutre apparentes que l'on trouve dans les villages de la Forêt d'Arden. Le château de Warwick (103), datant du Moyen-Age domine l'Avon. L'intérieur est du 17e siècle. Quelques-uns des anciens bâtiments de Covéntry subsistent, comme le long de Priory Row (104), près de la cathédrale. Stratford-upon-Avon (105) est surtout connu pour être le lieu de naissance de Shakespeare. Il y est enterré dans Trinity Church. Compton Wynyates (106) date du 16e siècle.

Das Moat House in Hampton-in-Arden (102) ist typisch für viele Häuser dieser Gegend. Das Schloß von Warwick (103) steht majestätisch auf einem steilen Felsen über dem Avon. Die im letzten Krieg verschont gebliebenen Häuser der Priory Row (104) in Coventry haben einen doppelten Überhang. Stratford-upon-Avon zieht jährlich Tausende von Menschen an. Shakespeare liegt in der Holy Trinity Church am Ufer des Avon (105) begraben. Compton Wynyates (106) ist ein Schaustück der Hausarchitektur dieses Landes.

104

105

Long before Shakespeare's time the great Forest of Arden extended to the north of the River Avon. There are a number of charming villages here which are redolent of the past. Both Henley-in-Arden, which Shakespeare is believed to have had in mind when writing *As You Like It*, and Hampton-in-Arden have many old timbered houses; the Moat House at Hampton-in-Arden (102) is a typical example. Warwick, the county town of its shire, has a history which can be traced back to A.D. 914 and its castle (103), standing majestically on a steep cliff overlooking the River Avon, is one of the best preserved medieval fortresses in the Midlands. The interior, dating chiefly from the seventeenth century, is truly magnificent. Not quite all of old Coventry was destroyed in the last war. Some of the ancient buildings were spared, and those that were repairable have been restored. In Priory Row (104) a narrow thoroughfare extending between the Cathedral and Trinity Street, the timber-framed buildings have a double overhang and are of seventeenth-century date. Few places in the British Isles have such a wide appeal as Stratford-upon-Avon, the birthplace of William Shakespeare who first saw the light of day in 1564 in a small house in Henley Street which is still a place of pilgrimage. He attended the local grammar-school and married Anne Hathaway when he was only eighteen. Shakespeare is buried in Holy Trinity Church on the banks of the Avon (105), and his memorial is in the sanctuary. Compton Wynyates (106) is one of the most beautiful examples of domestic architecture in the country. Since its completion early in the sixteenth century the main building has changed but little. The house is said to contain 80 rooms, 275 windows and 17 staircases and is noted for the number of secret passages it contains.

Gloucester Cathedral. 107.
La cathédrale de Gloucester. 107.
Der Dom von Gloucester. 107.

The South-West

Nine counties, grouped under the general title of the South-West, offer a variety of interest and scenic beauty. Some of Oxfordshire's southern boundary is formed by the Thames, whilst part of the beautiful region known as the Cotswolds is contained in the north of the county. Oxford itself has so much to offer that whole days may profitably be spent exploring that city. The western part of Berkshire, with its downs and river valleys, also belongs to the region of the south-west. The greater part of the Cotswolds lies in Gloucestershire. There is an intangible charm about the Cotswolds; the abundance of trees, the simple architecture of houses and cottages, built of warm-coloured local stone, the pleasant towns with their fine churches. Salisbury Plain, the Marlborough Downs and Savernake Forest give Wiltshire a spacious character, and Salisbury, with its cathedral, is of great interest. Within the county are the prehistoric monuments of Stonehenge and Avebury. Dorset, with its seventy miles of coast, has numbered many famous men among her seafarers, and her farmers are second to none. Gently rolling hills and secluded valleys watered by quiet little rivers combine to make the county one of the most pleasant of the south-west.

The counties of Somerset, Avon, Devon and Cornwall comprise one of the most beautiful areas in the whole of England. Somerset has within her borders the cliffs and caves of Cheddar and the wonderful cathedral city of Wells, whilst the county of Avon contains the Roman town of Bath and the historic city-port of Bristol. The great uplands of Dartmoor and Exmoor cover much of Devon, but the beauty of the two coasts attracts more visitors. The southern coast is a succession of delightful bays, coves and headlands, and the villages of the northern coast are finely situated. Cornwall shares with Devon the beauty of cove and bay, the fascination of moor and river. As befits a county with its roots deep in the past, Cornwall abounds in legend and romance, and few counties can boast such compelling coastal scenery.

108

109

110

Whitchurch dans l'Oxfordshire est un charmant village situé sur la Tamise, au pied des Chilterns. Magdalen College (109) est le premier des collèges d'Oxford sur la route de Londres. Il fut fondé au 15e siècle. Dans les parties de l'Oxfordshire restées rurales on trouve de petits villages pittoresques comme East Hagbourne (110). Abingdon (111) est sur la Tamise et l'on peut y visiter deux églises et la mairie datant de Charles II.

Whitchurch in Oxfordshire (108) am Fuß der Chilterns bietet einen herrlichen Anblick an der Themse. Das Magdalen College (109) ist das erste, das den Besucher von Oxford begrüßt. Sein Wahrzeichen ist der schöne Glockenturm mit dem Geläut von zehn Glocken. East Hagbourne (110) ist ein reizendes Dorf in dem noch unberührten Teil von Oxfordshire. Zwei bemerkenswerte Kirchen und das schöne Gebäude der County Hall zeichnen Abingdon (111) aus.

Whitchurch in Oxfordshire (108), one of nine places in England bearing this name, is most pleasantly situated on the River Thames at the foot of the Chilterns. Its principal mansion dates from Tudor times and its church is notable for its excellent brasses, one of which goes back to the early fifteenth century. In Whitchurch was born John Soane, the architect of the first Bank of England. Of all the Oxford colleges Magdalen (109) is the first to greet the visitor as he approaches the city along the London road. Founded by William of Waynflete in the fifteenth century, it incorporates part of the medieval hospital of St John which formerly occupied the site. The fine Bell Tower, containing a peal of ten bells, is a conspicuous landmark. The Great Hall has a Jacobean roof and cloisters surround the Great Quadrangle. There are many lovely villages tucked away in those parts of Oxfordshire which have escaped the hand of the 'developer'. Such a place is East Hagbourne (110), some five miles west of Wallingford. The village cross and the church are both old, the latter having arches of the thirteenth century. At Abingdon (111) the road from Henley crosses the Thames by a bridge, originally fifteenth century, but rebuilt in 1929. Two churches, St Helen's and St Nicholas', are both of considerable merit, but the finest building in the town is undoubtedly the County Hall, dating from the time of Charles II. Abingdon had an abbey in the sixth century, but only a medieval gateway and a few fragments remain.

111

Eastleach consists of twin villages separated by the River Leach which is spanned by an old stone foot-bridge, named 'Keble's Bridge' (112) in honour of the religious poet who was vicar here, and after whom Keble College at Oxford is named. Both Upper and Lower Slaughter are situated by a stream which finds its way into the River Windrush. In both villages several simple bridges, of both stone and timber, cross the stream. In the thirteenth-century church at Lower Slaughter (113) there is a most beautiful modern marble reredos depicting the Crucifixion. At Moreton-in-Marsh the old market-hall stands proudly in the centre of the main street, which forms part of the Roman Fosse Way. Old customs such as morris-dancing (114) survive in this and other Cotswold centres. Bibury (115) was described by William Morris as 'lying down in the winding valley beside the clear Coln'. The village is renowned for the wonderfully preserved row of fifteenth-century cottages known as Arlington Row. Salisbury Cathedral (116) has the distinction of posses-sing the tallest spire in England. This beautiful Early English building replaced the previous cathedral at Old Sarum, an Ancient British settlement on a near-by hill. Of particular interest are the Chapter House and the thirteenth-century cloister. Stonehenge (117) is probably the most important megalithic monu-ment in Britain. It dates from about 1500 B.C. and consisted originally of a complete circle of upright stones with lintels across each pair. Its purpose is not clearly understood, but it probably had both religious and astronomical connections.

113

116

114

Le poète religieux Keble a donné son nom au pont enjambant la Leach à Eastleach (112), reliant ainsi les deux moitiés du village. Les villages de Lower Slaughter (113) et Upper Slaughter sont construits le long de ruisseaux et parsemés de nombreux ponts. Les coutumes comme le Morris dancing (114) ont survécu dans les Cotswolds. Bibury (115) est connu pour ses cottages du 15e siècle. La cathédrale de Salisbury (116), construite sur le site de Old Sarum, a la flèche la plus haute d'Angleterre. Stonehenge (117) est un cercle de pierres dressées probablement lié à quelques rites religieux.

Eine alte Steinbrücke, Keble's Bridge (112), verbindet die Zwillingsdörfer von Eastleach. Einfache Stein- oder Holzbrücken führen auch über den Bach in Lower Slaughter (113). Der Moriskentanz ist einer der alten Bräuche von Moreton-in-Marsh (114). Das Dorf Bibury (115) ist bekannt wegen seiner Häuser der Arlington Row. Der Dom von Salisbury (116) besitzt neben dem höchsten Turm von England herrliche Kreuzgänge aus dem 13. Jahrhundert. Das Megalithmonument von Stonehenge (117) aus der Zeit um 1500 v. Chr. bildete ursprünglich einen riesigen Steinkreis.

117

115

118

Le village de Corfe Castle est très pittoresque et particulièrement connu pour les ruines du château (118) qui le domine. La côte du Dorset est très belle et l'érosion a façonné dans les roches tantôt tendres tantôt dures des formes étranges comme l'arche de Durdle Door (119). Les vallées, comme Doone Valley (120), allant à la mer à travers les landes d'Exmoor, sont appelées « coombes ». Elles furent rendues célèbres par les romans de Blackmore. La cathédrale de Wells (121) et les bâtiments qui l'entourent sont le vivant exemple de ce qu'était autrefois une ville ecclésiastique.

Das malerische Dorf Corfe Castle (118) wird von den Ruinen des Schlosses überragt. Die Küste von Dorset ist wegen ihrer Schönheit und der Vielfalt ihrer Felsformen berühmt. Besonders eindrucksvoll ist der natürliche Kalkbogen Durdle Door (119), der auch Scheunentor genannt wird. Mehrere der Talmulden, die aus dem Herzen von Exmoor zum Meer führen, werden mit dem in Blackmores Romanzen beschriebenen Doone Valley (120) gleichgesetzt Der Dom von Wells (121) und die unvergleichlichen Gebäude rings um ihn sind Ausdrucke dieser ehemals geistlich orientierten Stadt.

The village of Corfe Castle, though one of the most picturesque in Dorset, is most widely known for the castle ruins (118) which, standing on the top of a conical-shaped hill, completely dominate the village and the surrounding countryside, as the castle did a thousand years ago. The beautiful village sign commemorates an event which changed the course of English history, for it was here that Edward, the Martyr King of Wessex, was murdered at the instigation of his stepmother Elfrida in A.D. 978. The sea-coast of Dorset is famed for its beauty, and above all for the variety of its geological formations of hard and soft rocks. Where the sea has worn away the softer strata, there have been left many curiously shaped rocks and cliffs bearing quaint and picturesque names. One of the most impressive of these is to be found near Lulworth. It is named Durdle Door (119), or the Barndoor, and is a natural arch formed in the limestone cliff. The arch is large enough for a boat to sail through. From the heart of Exmoor many narrow valleys lead down to the sea. They bear the attractive West Country name of 'coombes'. This romantic part of Exmoor is the Doone country, made famous by Blackmore's romances. Several of the coombes have been identified with Doone Valley (120), but it is probable that Blackmore's valley is an imaginative composite, with details drawn from many of the coombes, but it is not difficult to visualise any of them peopled by the colourful characters which the novelist so vividly portrays. Wells Cathedral (121) and the incomparable group of buildings which surround it are unique. They stand today as a living example of the pattern of an ecclesiastical city such as it was when the Church was the supreme authority. A wonderful collection of carved figures, some of them larger than life-size, adorn the magnificent west front. The cathedral possesses an intricate mechanical clock, originally made by a monk of Glastonbury in the fourteenth century. Of particular interest is the Bishop's Palace which is surrounded by a moat.

119

121

120

Ilfracombe claims with some justice to be the perfect North Devon holiday resort. It is a town which has adapted itself to its hilly situation and is an excellent centre from which to explore the beauty spots of the region. The harbour (122), now chiefly used for fishing and pleasure craft, provided ships for the assault on Calais in the reign of Edward III. The coastal resorts of North and South Devon are separated by the great upland expanse of Dartmoor, a region particularly rich in historical relics. North Bovey (124), south of Moretonhampstead on the eastern edge of Dartmoor, is a most charming village. It has a famous inn, the Ring of Bells, a fine granite Perpendicular church and a stone cross which was once used as a footbridge across the River Bovey. The southern coast of Devon is a succession of delightful bays, coves and headlands. Torquay has a magnificent situation on the promontory which guards the northern end of Torbay. The harbour (123), consisting of an outer and inner basin, is framed by Waldon and Vane Hills. The Royal Duchy of Cornwall, the most westerly of English counties, consists of one large peninsula with two coasts. The southern coast, from Land's End to the Lizard, has earned itself the title of the 'Cornish Riviera'. Kynance Cove (125) lies about a mile from the Lizard, the most southerly point in Great Britain. The serpentine rock of which it is composed is carved into souvenirs by local craftsmen. The most striking natural feature of Newquay, the principal resort of the north-western coast, is the bold promontory of Towan Head which separates the eastern bay from the broad sweep of Pentire Sands and shelters the town from the force of Atlantic gales. The large eastern bay is divided into a number of smaller beaches; Tolcarne Beach (126) is one of the most popular. The Harbour (127) is the focal-point of St Ives, both for its activity and for the beauty of its setting. St Ives has a magnificent situation, bracing air and a picturesque old-world atmosphere.

122

123

124

125

126

127

Ilfracombe semble être le meilleur centre de villégiature de la côte nord du Devon. Son port (122) se consacre à la pêche et la navigation de plaisance. Dartmoor est la région riche en histoire s'étendant entre les côtes sud et nord du Devon; on y trouve de charmants villages comme North Bovey (124). Torquay est situé sur le promontoire nord de Torbay. Son port (123) est encadré de collines. Le Duché Royal de Cornouailles est le comté le plus à l'ouest d'Angleterre. Kynance Cove (125) est sur la côte sud aussi nommée la « Riviera de Cornouailles ». Newquay est remarquable pour le promontoire qui sépare les deux baies et protège la ville. La baie de l'est est coupée en petites plages comme celle de Tolcarne Beach (126). Le village de St Ives et son port (127) sont connus pour leur activité et leur pittoresque.

Ilfracombe ist ein ausgezeichneter Urlaubsort und Ausgangspunkt für Ausflüge in Devon. Der Hafen (122) wird jetzt hauptsächlich für Vergnügungsschiffahrt und Fischerei verwendet. North Bovey (124) mit seiner schönen Kirche im Perpendikelstil ist ein reizendes Dorf am Ostrand von Dartmoor. Die Südküste von Devon stellt eine Folge von entzückenden Buchten und Landzungen dar. Der Hafen von Torquay (123), der herrlich am nördlichen Vorsprung der Torbay liegt, besteht aus einem inneren und äußeren Becken. Die Küste Cornwalls zwischen Land's End und Lizard wird oft „Cornish Riviera" genannt; an ihr liegt Kynance Cove (125). Äußerst beliebt ist Tolcarne Beach (126) in der Ostbucht von Newquay. Der Hafen von St Ives (127) zeichnet sich durch rege Tätigkeit und durch große Schönheit aus.

The Scilly Isles, identified in Arthurian legend with Lyonnesse, lie about twenty-eight miles from the English mainland. They are reached from Penzance either by boat or by helicopter. In all the group comprises some 140 islands of which only five are inhabited. St Mary's is the largest, and Hugh Town the capital. Memorials to shipwrecked mariners are to be found in the churchyard in the Old Town. Typical of the small island settlements is New Grimsby (128) on Tresco which has a new abbey on the site of a Benedictine priory of the tenth century. Relics of the Civil War, in which the Scillies played a notable part, are to be found in the remains of seventeenth-century castles. The other inhabited islands are St Martins, St Agnes and Bryler. Prehistoric remains testify to the fact that some of the islands were inhabited in far-off days. The Isles of Scilly enjoy a particularly mild climate and the principal occupation is the growing of early spring flowers which are sent in large quantities to the principal markets of the mainland. Naturalists, too, find much to interest them, especially ornithologists, for numerous varieties of sea-birds breed along the coasts.

Les îsles Scilly sont á vingt-huit milles de la côte. Le climat y est très doux. Cinq sont habitées; St Mary, la plus grande, St Martin's, St Agnes, Bryher et Tresco. Le village de new Grimsby (128) est un example de l'habitat local.

Nur fünf der 140 Scilly Inseln sind bewohnt. New Grimsby (128) auf Tresco ist typisch für die kleinen Siedlungen. Durch das milde Klima sind die Inseln ideal für Blumenzucht. Die Küsten sind Brutstätte vieler Arten von Seevögeln.